ALL YOU CAN BE

Dwight Howard

with **John Denton**

Illustrated by Children from the Boys & Girls Clubs of Central Florida

TRIUMPH
BOOKS

Hey wooooooooooorld!

That phrase has stuck with me since I first started playing in the NBA seven years ago. I even have it printed on a lot of my Adidas shoes for inspiration. It is my motto, my motivation to work hard and make a difference every day.

Let me start off by saying that while you probably know me as a basketball player, I am so much more than that. The stuff I do off the court is just as important as the dunks, blocked shots, and rebounds I make for the Orlando Magic.

Through the NBA and the Boys & Girls Clubs, I have worked closely with a lot of kids like you over the years. I love talking to them about what they want to be when they grow up. I wanted to write this book to encourage all kids to follow their dreams. I learned at an early age that

if I planned out my goals, put in the work necessary, and made sacrifices, anything in this world was within reach.

Children from the Boys & Girls Clubs of Central Florida provided the illustrations you will see in this book. It's inspiring to see their dreams come to life in the form of art. With hard work, strong education, and focus, you can make your dreams come true.

Even when kids tell me that they want to play in the NBA and take my job someday, I stress to them that they have to have more in their life than a love of sports. The way I look at it is this: Basketball players—even ones who make all-star teams and appear in commercials—come and go through the years. But the ones who are remembered

forever are the ones who make a difference off the court. That's why I've always tried to broaden my horizons and do all I can away from basketball. I want to create that kind of lasting legacy. It is a way for me to give thanks for all of the blessings I have had in my life.

So I hope you all enjoy my first book and that it inspires you to reach for your dreams. I started out as a skinny kid from Atlanta and went on to become the NBA's "Superman." If I can do it, you can do it, too. Whatever your goal is, dream big and work hard!

—Dwight Howard

ARTIST: **Essence Seabrook**

Laying the Foundation

I was born on December 8, 1985, in a town just outside of Atlanta, Georgia. My mother, Sheryl Howard, and father, Dwight Howard Sr., tried several times to have another kid after my two sisters came along, but something went wrong each time. When I finally arrived, my mother called me her "little miracle baby." Little did my mom know that her "little" baby was going to grow up and be 6'11" and weigh 275 pounds.

My parents were really strict, but they were always fair. They treated me with love and respect, but I had to act right and do right—or else. My mom worked at the courthouse and later became a teacher. My dad was a Georgia State Trooper, so that's where his discipline came from. He always wanted us to have our school uniforms ironed the night before and set out for the following morning.

My parents were even stricter when it came to education. If I ever misbehaved, my dad would show up at the school. My mother became the P.E. teacher at our school when I was in middle school. It was fun having her there every day with me, and I think she liked being there to stay close to me.

I might not have always understood at the time why my parents kept such a close eye on me and were tough on me, but I understand it now. Their love—sometimes it was tough love—laid a foundation of discipline and respect.

Having two strong parents at home and at school helped to make me the person that

I am now. I don't know where I would be without them. I know not everyone out there has two parents at home, but you should still always listen to them and do what they say because they know what they are talking about. Trust

Georgia. It was a nice neighborhood, and close to our church and my school. All my friends and I did growing up was play basketball and hang out at the house. I got my toughness from being on the basketball court. As a kid, I was usually the smallest one out there. (Hard to believe now, isn't it?)

If guys were going to play on the court at my house, they had to follow the rules or they couldn't play there. Although I was short

Having parents who care about you and stay involved in your day-to-day activities is a very good thing.

me when I say this: Having parents who care about you and stay invloved in your day-to-day activities is a very good thing.

I lived in two different types of neighborhoods when I was growing up. The first place was on Godby Road in College Park, Georgia. It was kind of a rough area, but because my dad was a state trooper and had his police car parked in the driveway, we never really had any problems. When I was 16 years old and in high school, we moved to an area in East Point,

and skinny, I was always determined not to let anyone push me around on my home court. It was a physical game, but we didn't call many fouls. That prepared me for what I would face in the NBA against the other big guys.

I didn't go out much when I was a kid other than to school or to play basketball. Mom was the one who would usually get mad if I stayed out late. Once, four or five of my friends came to my house to stay overnight. We went out to the movies but didn't come home until 4:00 in the

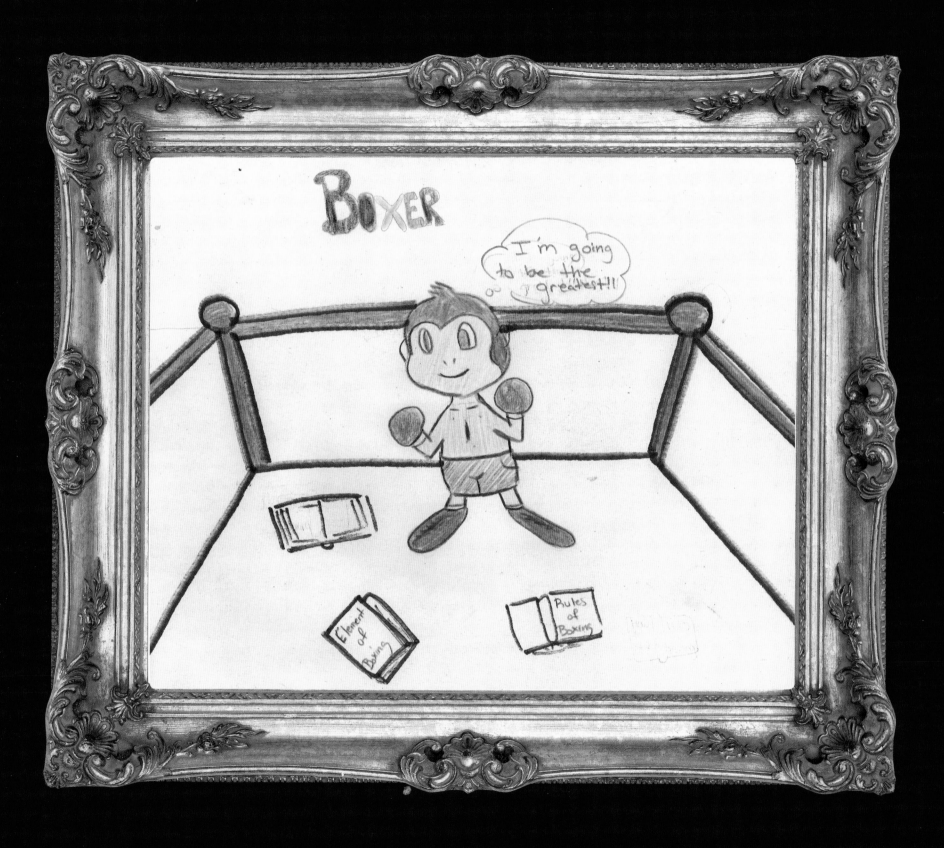

ARTIST: **Zha'Niko McMillan**

ARTIST: **Amanda C. DeJesus**

morning! When we finally got home, my cousin Kevin Samples unlocked the door for us at the house, to our relief. But my mom was sitting on the couch waiting for us, so when we walked into the room she jumped up and busted us!

My friends stayed at my house a lot when we were in high school, and when they did they had to follow the rules of our house. We were in big trouble for not following her rules that time.

I've always found that the best friends are the ones who care about you as a person, not about what you can do for them. When I first got down to Orlando as an NBA player, the only people that I really knew were my teammates and my cousin, Kevin. I really had to pray for some friends in my life. Luckily, I was able to find four or five friends from my church, and we've been tight ever since. I don't even consider them friends anymore; they are like my brothers.

One of my best friends in the whole world, James, has known me since I was a skinny little kid. He was friends with my brother when we were growing up. Then he went off to school in Daytona Beach, near Orlando. When I came to the Magic, James would come down and see me every weekend in Orlando and we would chill, hang out, and talk. Our relationship grew into the bond that it is now. I'd do anything in the

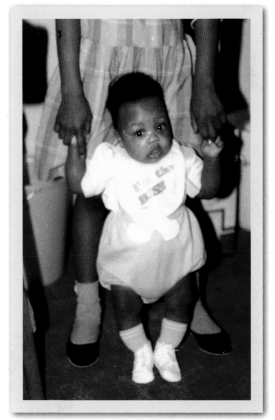

It is important to pick your friends wisely.

world for him and I know that he'd do the same for me, too.

It is important to pick your friends wisely. Some people think that having a lot of friends is good. But having a small group of friends who you trust and who know you inside and out is even better. Friendship provides some of the best memories of your life. My buddies and I still talk about the fun times we used to have back in the day when we were young and silly.

Sometimes the people you hang out with can have a negative impact on you. Some people want to see you fail in life. Running with the wrong crowd can sometimes get you in a lot of trouble.

That's why it's so important that you pick and choose your friends carefully. If they are good people and believe in a lot of the same things that you do, you'll likely be friends for life and they will always be there for you. But if they are getting in trouble, dragging you down, and don't want to see you succeed in life, then you need to move on and find new friends. Sometimes, it's just that simple. •

ARTIST: **Asia Newsome**

ARTIST: **Dequan Felder**

Big Smiles & Big Dreams

As far back as I can remember, people have always remarked on my big ol' cheesy smile. People sometimes tell me that my smile can light up a room like a Christmas tree. It doesn't matter if I'm angry, frustrated, tired, or happy—I've always got a smile on my face. It's just who I am, I guess.

Smiling has always been my way of greeting people. I've found through my 25 years on this earth that by smiling I can make other people smile, too—and *I love making people smile!* I try to keep my teammates laughing in the locker room, on the bus, or flying to the next city on the airplane. If I wasn't a basketball player, I really think I would have made it in Hollywood as an actor because I love to put on

a show for people. I can imitate a lot of funny voices. I recently visited *The Tonight Show with Jay Leno,* and I did my impressions of Charles Barkley ("That's tuuuurrrrrr-ible") and Arnold Schwarzenegger. I had the audience laughing pretty hard.

Sports Illustrated actually did a story on me a couple of years ago that criticized me for smiling so much on the court. They wondered if somebody like me who liked to have so much fun could ever win a championship. That really bothered me.

What they clearly didn't understand about me is that I play my best out on the court when I'm having fun. I can still be intense and physical and play with a smile. Some people take it as being "soft" or "weak" when you smile on the court, but I think you can ask the guys who guard me every night and they will tell you that that is anything but the case. I bring my intensity and focus to every game and I can deliver some pretty hard blows to people out on the court, but I like to go into games with a clear mind. Every time that I've gone into a game upset, I usually didn't play well because my attention was off the game and on something else.

I'm able to be freer when I'm smiling and having fun, whether I'm on or off the court. When I meet kids, that's the first message I want to send. Just because I'm a big guy in stature doesn't mean that I'm a mean person. I want people to know they can have fun with me.

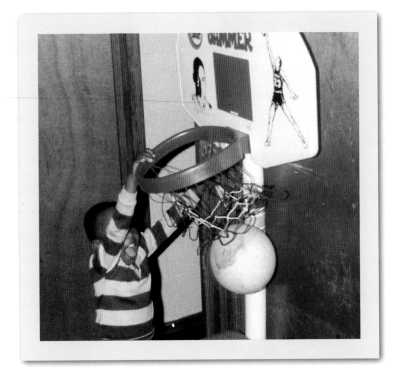

My dreams are as big as my smiles. It's so important for you to set dreams, to aim high, and to work hard to accomplish your goals. Take me as an example: I was just a skinny country boy from Atlanta who dreamed of not only playing in the NBA, but of someday being the first overall pick in the NBA Draft. Remarkably, that dream came true. But it was because I put in the work and never let anything distract me from what I wanted to achieve.

As far back as I can remember, I was always around basketball. My mom, who was on the first-ever women's basketball team at Morris Brown College, made sure there was always some kind of ball in my crib when I was a baby.

I remember learning to dribble a ball out back at my house when I was just three years old. Even now, I still look back at the pictures of me dunking a ball on a Nerf hoop. It's crazy, but those dunks on the little plastic goal look exactly like the dunks I make now in the NBA.

When we moved to East Point, people began to tell me that I was too skinny to ever make it to the NBA and that the school I attended, Southwest Atlanta Christian Academy, was too small for scouts to notice me. They said that because I played at a Christian school, I was too

ARTIST: **Aisha Benoit-Jean**

ARTIST: **Antonia LeDestiny McCree-Burton**

soft to play big-time basketball. Some people are discouraged by negative talk, but I used it as fuel to succeed.

The first time I really felt as if I could make it to the NBA was in the eighth grade. I was outside playing basketball on a tennis court against some older guys. They didn't want me to play because they thought I was too little, but I wanted that challenge of playing against the older kids. They were two of the best guys in my school at the time—Mike Danks and Chris Prothro—but I kept taking them to the post and scoring every time. Those two guys were big and strong, but I just dominated them. My teammate kept telling me, "You're going to the NBA out of high school. I can already see it in you." That was the first time anybody said that to me, and it opened my eyes and made me believe in myself. After hearing it said out loud, I really felt like I could do it.

Not long after that day, I wrote out a list of all of my goals and dreams and put it up on my bedroom wall. The first thing on the list was to be the first pick in the 2004 NBA Draft. At the time, people thought I was crazy for writing

that down because most kids didn't go from high school to the NBA, let alone as the first pick. That didn't matter to me. Every night before I went to bed I would look at that list, and I'd dream about getting to the NBA all night long.

Of course, it didn't hurt my chances of getting to the NBA when I grew almost seven inches during my freshman year of high school. I went from 6'2" to almost 6'9"! My mom was mad at me because I was growing so fast that I kept getting too tall for my pants. We were constantly buying new pants and new shoes for my long legs and growing feet. The "little miracle baby" was growing up really fast—and nobody around me could believe it!

Just before my big growth spurt, another big moment in my basketball life happened. When I was in the eighth grade—I was about 6'0" then—I dunked a basketball for the first time. Man, was I ever hooked on it after that! I guess I haven't stopped dunking since.

I worked on it all year. I knew that to be able to dunk a basketball you have to be able to dunk a tennis ball first, so I started with that. I

17

had to be able to get my wrist over the rim with the tennis ball before I could even think about dunking a basketball. I practiced, practiced, and practiced some more.

Finally, my big moment came in our student vs. teacher basketball game at the end of the year. I learned from all of that practice that the easiest place to dunk is on the side of the rim rather than the front. I got a breakaway in the game, went up to the hoop, and did a two-handed dunk. Everyone in the crowd went absolutely crazy! If I remember it right, I don't even think the rim moved or the net shook when I dunked it. I'll never forget that moment—the school was cheering and over the sound system, "Hip Hop Hooray" was blaring. I remember it like it was yesterday.

In high school at Southwest Atlanta Christian Academy, I constantly worked on my skills and grew into a pretty good basketball player. Before my senior year, there was a debate among scouts. Some people thought Al Jefferson in Mississippi was the best high school player, and some people thought it was me. Jefferson and I played against each other in an AAU (Amateur Athletic Union) tournament and guess I got the best of him that time. It put a lot of focus on me in my senior season. (Al went on to make it to the NBA, too. We still laugh about those high school days.)

Nobody believes me now, but I played center, forward, and guard in high school. My idols growing up were Michael Jordan and Magic Johnson because I saw myself as a player who could do it all the same way those players did it for their teams. I used to be that 6'11"guy breaking the press by dribbling the ball up the court.

As a senior in high school, I averaged 25 points, 18 rebounds, eight blocks, and three assists per game and our team won the Class A Georgia State High School Championship. By the way, winning that state championship was the second item on the list that I taped to my bedroom wall.

Accomplishing that goal showed me that anything was possible in basketball as long as I set my mind to it and kept my sights on it. A lot of colleges came after me after my senior year, and I committed to play at the University of North Carolina, but all of those schools knew that I already had my mind made up to go to the NBA. *Playing in the NBA and being selected as the first pick was my goal. I wasn't going to let anything stop me from achieving that.*

That drive and determination prepared me for the next stage of my life. •

ARTIST: **Makayla Gadsden**

ARTIST: **Anthony Kumar**

A Magical Ride

June 24, 2004, will go down as one of the happiest nights of my life. It was the night that the Orlando Magic made me the No. 1 overall pick in the NBA Draft. I fulfilled my top goal, the aspiration that I set all the way back in eighth grade when I was just 13 years old.

I still remember that night in New York City. I wore a blue suit, a light blue shirt, and a blue tie, hoping that the Magic would pick me. I wanted to shake NBA commissioner David Stern's hand and put on that blue Magic cap to match my blue outfit.

I wanted to be that No. 1 pick so much. But all the work and preparation was over. It was out of my hands. I was just a country boy from Atlanta up in New York City, giving interviews alongside older college players. Looking back on it now I can laugh, but at the time I was so nervous.

I remember sitting off to the side of ESPN's analysts with some of the other players. I don't think they knew that we could hear everything that they were saying. They speculated that the first overall pick was between me, the high school kid who not many people knew, and Emeka Okafor, who had just won a college national championship at Connecticut. The guys at ESPN, especially Dick Vitale, thought that the high school kids in the draft wouldn't perform at the NBA level. Vitale even said that the Magic would regret passing on Okafor if they drafted me.

When Commissioner Stern announced my name as the first pick, a wave of emotions rushed over me. I was happy for myself and my family. I felt blessed that God had allowed me to reach my goal. And I was happy that *all of my hard work, sacrificing, dreaming, and praying had paid off.*

As it turned out, I was the last high school player ever to be taken No. 1 overall in the NBA Draft. The league changed the rule in 2005, requiring players to be at least 19 years old and/or one year out of high school. Kwame

Brown in 2001, LeBron James in 2003, and I are the only players ever to be picked first overall straight out of high school.

My first couple teams with the Magic weren't too good, and we missed the playoffs in both 2005 and 2006. I put up pretty good numbers my first two years in the NBA, although my first coach, Johnny Davis, never ran any plays designed for me. He would always say that if I wanted the ball, I'd have to go and rebound it off the glass. I didn't like that at the time, but I think it helped me become the rebounder that I am today.

When I was drafted by the Magic I weighed 240 pounds—pretty skinny by NBA standards. I lifted weights, but I could never put on much mass. When I was a kid, my doctor told me that one day I would be able to gain weight and the muscles would catch up to my body. I was so eager for

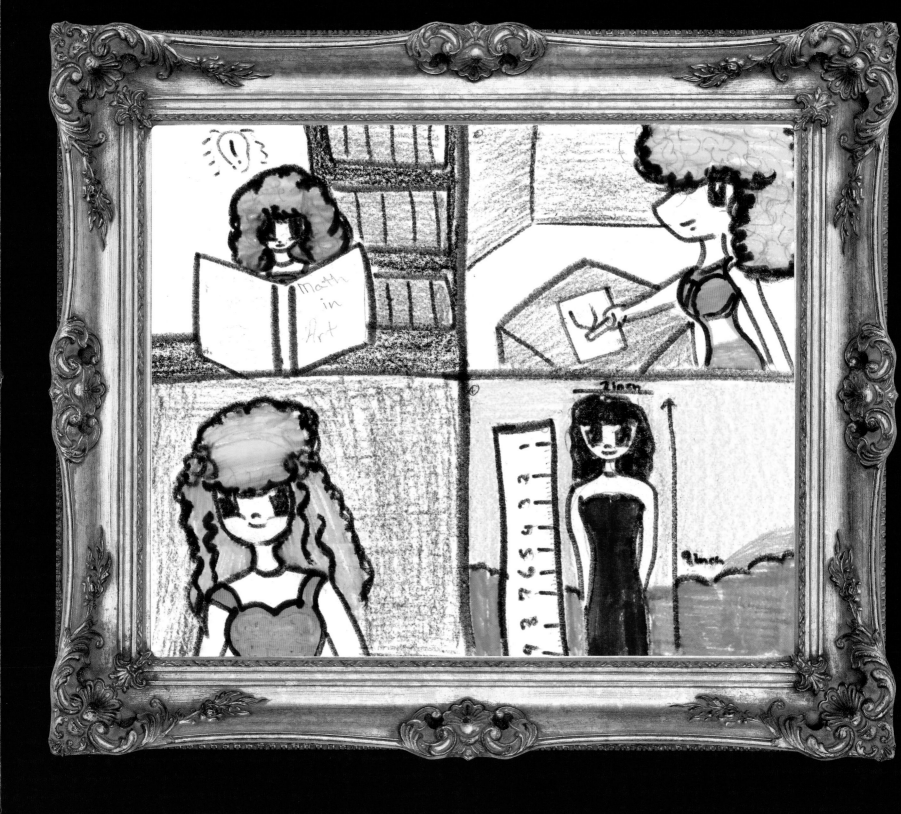

ARTIST: **Aaliyah Tucker**

ARTIST: **Mya Bagwell**

that to happen, but everybody just thought I was this skinny, lanky basketball player with no strength.

In my first two years in the NBA I committed myself to staying in the weight room

That discipline is the reason why I have the body that I have now. It didn't come without a lot of hard work, sweat, and tears. God has blessed me with my height and an ability to jump, but none of my success in basketball would have

The way I see it, playing sports has taught me a lot of very important life lessons.

and working on my body. And over time—and after eating steak and potatoes at every meal—I finally started growing into the beast that I am today.

During my first year in the NBA, guys would hold me so I couldn't move or break free. The first time that Atlanta Hawks power forward Kevin Willis and I squared off stuck with me for a long time. Kevin was ripped with muscles and was considered one of the strongest guys in the league. I tried to hit him at his waist and block him out, but he took his arm and clamped down on mine—they call it "the chicken wing"—and I couldn't move at all. I remember thinking, *I'm not ever going to let anybody do this to me again in a game.* I stuck to my diet and kept at it in the weight room and eventually it paid off.

come without the work that I put in. That work goes all the way back to when I was that skinny eighth-grade kid trying to dunk for the first time. It didn't happen until I practiced over and over and kept working at it.

I have learned to be mentally and physically tough. I've learned to persevere and to push myself further than I thought was humanly possible.

One of the very first things I learned was sacrifice. If you want to be great at something you have to pay the price and sacrifice. (Hey, that rhymes! I crack myself up sometimes.)

There were a lot of times growing up when I had to sacrifice things in life. I'd want to go out with my friends, go to the movies or do things like a normal teenager, but I knew if I

did that I'd be taking myself away from bettering my basketball skill set. Instead, I stayed in the gym.

I was even able to turn one of the low points of my basketball life into a big-time positive with some good old-fashioned hard work. When I was in the eighth grade, I went up and tried to dunk on somebody but he ran up under me. I landed on my left wrist and broke it. I wore a cast for several weeks.

Most people don't know that I was 100 percent left-handed growing up as a kid. But after breaking my left wrist, my right hand was the only one I could use. So for hours and hours,

I would work on hook shots, layups, and free throws with my right hand. Little did I know back then that being ambidextrous would help me in the NBA. But I was able to better my right-handed moves by turning the broken wrist from a negative into a positive.

You need great discipline to prevent things from coming between you and your goals in life. Sprinkle in some confidence, a little bit of talent, and a strong faith, and you can accomplish anything. •

ARTIST: **Tykeria Fryar**

ARTIST: **Destiny King**

Breaking Through

In 2008 and 2009, everything started coming together for me in a big way. I began to be recognized as an elite player. I finally felt like the skinny kid from Atlanta with all of the big dreams was on his way to reaching everything that he wanted out of basketball.

Because I went straight from high school to the NBA, I knew there would be a short transition time for me to get used to playing against older men. But because I was determined and willing to put in the work, I always knew that I was on a collision course to be a great, All-NBA player.

The 2008 All-Star Game was the launching pad of sorts for my alter ego, Superman. It was at the slam dunk contest that year that I first put on the Superman cape and leaped tall buildings in a single bound. Having the chance to impersonate Superman had been a dream of mine since I was a kid. I've always thought Superman is just the coolest dude on the planet. (I just wish I had his X-ray vision!)

I've done a lot of crazy things through the years on the basketball court—reached 13 feet high on the backboard, kissed the rim, and dunked on a 12½' goal—but the "Superman

dunk," as people still call it, was amazing to me. Every time that I see it today on the replays, it still brings goose bumps to my body because it's a thing of beauty. I never imagined that I could jump that high, and seeing myself do it was just amazing. And the reaction that the dunk got when I soared through the air and got up high enough to throw it through the rim made it even more special. People have told me that will go down as one of the greatest dunks of all time, right up there with Dr. J jumping from the free-throw line and Michael Jordan's "Rock the Cradle" dunk. I consider it a tremendous honor to be in that company.

After that, it seemed like everyone knew who I was overnight. *It's amazing how one moment can change your life.* We went on to have great success that season with the Magic, winning a playoff series for the first time in 12 years. I had three 20-point, 20-rebound games in that series against Toronto, and it gave me the confidence and paved the way for what came next in my career.

I was chosen to be a part of the Team USA national squad in 2006 with an eye toward the 2008 Summer Olympics in Beijing, China. Team USA had struggled in the 2004 Olympics. A group of the best players in the NBA were recruited to help put America back on top in basketball and win the gold medal.

ARTIST: **Aikia D'zariyah Highsmith**

ARTIST: **Jazmin Geathers**

The 1996 Olympic squad was known as "the Dream Team," and we were known as "the Redeem Team." I've never seen a group of guys more determined to scratch, claw, and fight for something in my life. We all were so proud to be representing our country, and there was just no way that we were going to leave China without that gold medal.

Before I left for China, I got a taste of what representing my country would be like. A few weeks before the Olympics, I was working out at Jones High School in Orlando, running on the track at 7:00 in the morning. People were gathered around, encouraging me, "Come on Dwight. You have to do this for America." They were chanting, "USA! USA! USA!" Some of the people there were even running with me to push me through the sprints.

During the Olympic Games, all I could think about was those people and how I wanted to bring home the gold for them. At first, I was kind of upset that I wasn't the guy who scored the points for our team, but then I realized that it wasn't my role. After I got a better understanding of what my job was, I just relaxed and did what I was supposed to do to the best of my ability.

Winning that gold medal meant everything to me. I didn't let that thing out of my sight for a couple of months after we got home. I used to carry the medal around with me everywhere I went—even on road trips with the Magic.

Every time I would look at that shiny gold medal I would think back to those days growing up in Atlanta when I dreamed about being a basketball star. It really put into perspective all of the hard work and days of sacrifice I put in to get to that point. I was proud of myself for being willing to work and keeping my focus so that my dreams would become a reality.

The 2008–09 NBA season brought another career-defining moment for me. Orlando is considered very small-market as far as NBA cities go, and we don't often get credit for being an elite team. It's gotten better in the last couple years, but it still feels that way sometimes.

When I first got to the Magic, when people thought of Orlando, they thought of Walt Disney World. Around town, nobody was talking about the Magic. You didn't see that many Magic jerseys, flags, or bumper stickers on the cars. My teammate and close friend Jameer Nelson and I made a vow to one another that we were going to change that and put the Magic on the map nationwide.

We finally did that with our playoff run in 2009. Many picked us to lose in the first round to the 76ers—especially after we lost

Game 1—but we went on to beat Philadelphia. Then nobody gave us a chance at all to beat the defending champs, the Boston Celtics, in the second round, but we came back from a 3–2 deficit to beat Boston in Game 7 on their home court.

In the Eastern Conference Finals that year, we were huge—I repeat, huge—underdogs against Cleveland and LeBron James. Early in that series, I showed that I meant business when I dunked so hard that the shot clock broke off the backboard. We won that series in six games. I keep a framed picture in my house of me holding the Eastern Conference Championship trophy.

That win put us in the NBA Finals opposite the Los Angeles Lakers. I was so honored to be playing at that level. Getting to the NBA Finals might be the greatest thing I've ever accomplished in basketball. There are so many great players who compete their whole careers and never make it to the Finals, so I was just so thrilled to be there at that summit, playing on the game's biggest stage.

The Lakers won the championship. We lost two overtime games in that series, and that haunted me throughout the off-season. There are times even now when I wonder, had we done this or that differently, if things might have gone the opposite way. Then I'd have a big ol' shiny championship ring on my finger—and, of course, a big ol' smile to match.

After we lost to the Lakers, Jameer Nelson and I stayed out on the bench to watch Los Angeles celebrate and get their trophy. We wanted that pain seared into our minds so that it would drive us to work hard to get back again the next season. While getting to the Finals was one of the greatest accomplishments of my basketball life, it doesn't replace not winning it.

I cried more after that game than I had since my days in high school. Back when I was in high school, I'd cry after every loss. In the NBA, people told me that I couldn't get so emotional after each game because we play so many of them. But losing to the Lakers hurt me so much. I don't know if you ever get over falling in the Finals until you win a championship someday.

Remember that list that I had over my bed with my goals written down when I was a kid? Now there's a new list and it has just one item on it. It's a picture of the gold NBA Championship Trophy. That's my ultimate goal, and I won't stop until I get it. •

ARTIST: **Denisha Culver**

ARTIST: **Sharlan Surjan**

Giving Back

I've always felt that I was put on this earth by God to do special things. And I'm not talking about just on the basketball court.

I have been so blessed in life and I feel that I have a responsibility to give back to the others around me. That's why when I'm not playing for the Magic, I'm usually very active in my community, doing what I can to help out others.

There are a lot of ways to show that we are grateful. Some people do that by just giving away money, which can be really helpful in some situations. But I enjoy spending time with people, taking pictures and having fun. *Spending time with people can often be the best thing you can do for somebody.* Giving them a gift might make them feel good in that moment, but in my experience, people will always remember the

Never let anybody tell you what you can't do, or change you as a person.

time you spent with them more than anything else. Taking time out to show people that you truly care is something meaningful and lasting.

I want to encourage you guys out there to do the same thing. You might not be an NBA player, but you can make a difference in your neighborhood with your actions and your time.

I am often asked how I got to where I am now. I always say that while the good Lord has blessed me with talent, it takes a lot more than that to be successful.

It was important for me to dream big when I was a kid, but I had to back up those dreams with a lot of hard work, sacrifice, and focus. You have to hold onto your dreams. Don't let anyone tell you that you can't do it.

I still think back to when I was growing up in Atlanta and they told me that I was too skinny to ever make it to the NBA. And I think back to those ESPN announcers who said it would be a mistake for the Magic to select me first overall in the NBA Draft. Even today, that stuff drives me and motivates me.

Never let anybody tell you what you can't do, or change who you are as a person. At times, I used to let what people say affect how I act, but I don't do that anymore. What matters is that you believe in yourself, not what others think about you or your potential.

I've been to five NBA All-Star Games, I have a gold medal, I've been to the NBA Finals, I've won the NBA's Defensive Player of the Year

ARTIST: **Aliyah Hobbs**

ARTIST: **Tiana Peters**

award twice, and I won the slam dunk contest, and you know what? I practice harder now than I ever have. All of that success has just made me hungrier.

It's great to be happy with your success, but you have to also push, scrap, and fight for more out of life. It wouldn't be okay for me to say I've made a few All-Star teams, played in the NBA Finals, and then just quit. That's not what great players and great people do in life. They are always searching and looking for ways to be better and make themselves better in life and their professions.

I always tell myself to not be satisfied with having a little bit of success because a lot is better than a little. My goal every day when I wake up is to strive to be better and get every last ounce out of my ability. If I don't achieve everything that's possible for me in life I will be disappointed with myself. That's why I keep on pushing myself and expecting more and more out of myself.

The way I see it, my best is still yet to come. It's been a wild ride so far, and I'm eager to see where this life takes me next. Peace out.

—Dwight Howard

Dream Big!

I wish we could have included them all! Here are a few more great illustrations from kids dreaming big.

ARTIST: **Kaiden Posatis**

ARTIST: **Kaliah Sinclair Harvey**

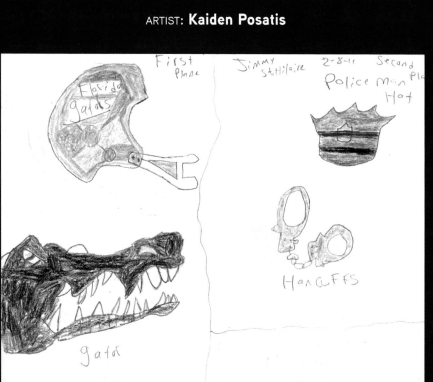

ARTIST: **Jimmy St. Hilaire**

ARTIST: **Zamarea Vigilance**

ARTIST: **Ashanti Miller**

ARTIST: **Elizabeth Pamphile**

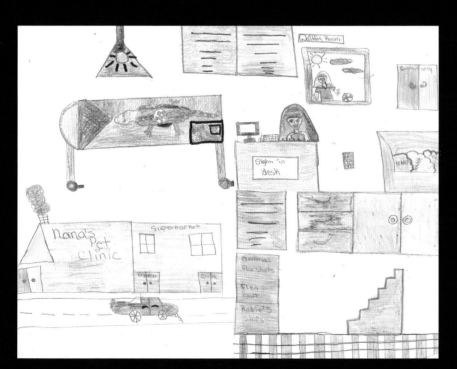

ARTIST: **Shanese Rodriguez**

ARTIST: **Chasity Pugh**

This book is available in quantity at special discounts for your group or organization. For further information, contact:

Triumph Books
542 South Dearborn Street
Suite 750
Chicago, Illinois 60605
312. 939. 3330
Fax 312. 663. 3557
www.triumphbooks.com
Printed in China
ISBN: 978-1-60078-414-9

Design by Paul Petrowsky

Family photos courtesy of the author. All other photos courtesy of AP Images.

Illustrated by Children from the Boys & Girls Clubs of Central Florida

Published in cooperation with the Boys & Girls Clubs of Central Florida

BOYS & GIRLS CLUBS
OF CENTRAL FLORIDA